TENNESSEE

Pamela McDowell

www.av2books.com

LET'S READ
AV²
BY WEIGL™
ADDED VALUE • AUDIO VISUAL

Go to **www.av2books.com**, and enter this book's unique code.

BOOK CODE

A 4 7 6 4 8 0

AV² by Weigl brings you media enhanced books that support active learning.

AV² provides enriched content that supplements and complements this book. Weigl's AV² books strive to create inspired learning and engage young minds in a total learning experience.

Your AV² Media Enhanced books come alive with...

Audio
Listen to sections of the book read aloud.

Video
Watch informative video clips.

Embedded Weblinks
Gain additional information for research.

Try This!
Complete activities and hands-on experiments.

Key Words
Study vocabulary, and complete a matching word activity.

Quizzes
Test your knowledge.

Slide Show
View images and captions, and prepare a presentation.

... and much, much more!

Published by AV² by Weigl
350 5th Avenue, 59th Floor
New York, NY 10118
Website: www.av2books.com   www.weigl.com

Library of Congress Cataloging-in-Publication Data

McDowell, Pamela.
  Tennessee / Pamela McDowell.
     p. cm. -- (Explore the U.S.A.)
  Includes bibliographical references and index.
  ISBN 978-1-61913-405-8 (hard cover : alk. paper)
  1. Tennessee--Juvenile literature. I. Title.
  F436.3.M353 2013
  976.8--dc23
                          2012016264

Printed in the United States of America in North Mankato, Minnesota
1 2 3 4 5 6 7 8 9   16 15 14 13 12

052012
WEP040512

Project Coordinator: Karen Durrie
Art Director: Terry Paulhus

Weigl acknowledges Getty Images as the primary image supplier for this title.

TENNESSEE

Contents

2   AV² Book Code
4   Nickname
6   Location
8   History
10 Flower and Seal
12 Flag
14 Animal
16 Capital
18 Goods
20 Fun Things to Do
22 Facts
24 Key Words

3

This is Tennessee.
It is called the Volunteer State.
Soldiers from Tennessee
volunteered in the War of 1812.

This is the shape of Tennessee. It is in the south part of the United States.

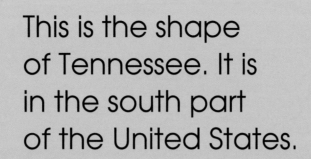

Where is Tennessee?

Canada

Pacific Ocean

United States

Atlantic Ocean

Mexico

Tennessee is bordered by eight states.

People have lived in Tennessee for more than 11,000 years. American Indians grew crops and lived near the rivers that flow through the state.

American Indians made large mounds in Tennessee.

9

The purple iris is the Tennessee state flower. Irises can be used to make perfume.

The Tennessee state seal has a cotton plant, a plow, and wheat.

The seal also shows a riverboat.

This is the state flag of Tennessee. It has a blue circle with three white stars.

The stars stand for the mountains, hills, and valleys in Tennessee.

The state animal of Tennessee is the raccoon. Raccoons are good climbers. They often live in trees.

Explorer Davy Crockett was known for wearing a raccoon hat.

This is the state capital of Tennessee. It is named Nashville.

Nashville is nicknamed Music City.

Maple, oak, and cedar trees grow in Tennessee. These trees are used to make lumber.

Tennessee makes the most pencils in the United States.

Tennessee is known for music.

People from around the world come to visit music museums and hear concerts.

TENNESSEE FACTS

These pages provide detailed information that expands on the interesting facts found in the book. These pages are intended to be used by adults as a learning support to help young readers round out their knowledge of each state in the *Explore the U.S.A.* series.

Pages 4–5

Tennessee has many nicknames, including the Big Bend State and the Hog State. The most popular nickname is the Volunteer State. Volunteer soldiers fought against the British in the Battle of New Orleans in 1812. They were led by General Andrew Jackson, who became the 7th president of the United States in 1829.

Pages 6–7

On June 1, 1796, Tennessee joined the United States as the 16th state. It shares its borders with Kentucky, Virginia, North Carolina, Georgia, Alabama, Mississippi, Arkansas, and Missouri. Tennesseans are often called Butternuts. During the Civil War, Tennessee soldiers who joined the Confederate States Army were given the name because of the tan color of their uniforms.

Pages 8–9

About 2,000 years ago, the Woodland people built large mounds to use for ceremonies and burial. Many of these mounds can still be seen in parts of the state. The largest is Saul's Mound at Pinson Mounds State Archaeological Park. Cherokee, Chickasaw, and Yuchi American Indian tribes also settled near Tennessee rivers long ago.

Pages 10–11

There are 300 different species of iris. The word *iris* comes from the Greek word for rainbow because of the many different colors of irises. The plow, wheat sheaf, and cotton plant on the state seal are symbols of Tennessee agriculture. The boat shows the importance of rivers to Tennessee's economy.

Pages 12–13

The state flag's three stars represent Tennessee's Great Smoky Mountains, its highlands, and the Cumberland Plateau. Two official salutes were written for the flag. The first salute is "Three white stars on a field of blue, God keep them strong and ever true, It is with pride and love that we, Salute the Flag of Tennessee."

Pages 14–15

In the 1800s and early 1900s, thousands of raccoons were killed each year for their fur. Frontiersman Davy Crockett, who was born in Tennessee, made "coonskin caps" popular. The number of raccoons in the state declined for a time, but has grown in recent years. The raccoon was declared Tennessee's state animal in 1971.

Pages 16–17

Nashville's original name was Nashborough. More than 600,000 people live in Nashville. The city is home to the Grand Ole Opry, the world's longest-running live radio program. The Opry features country music performers. Nashville has many recording studios. Musicians from around the world come to Nashville to make records.

Pages 18–19

Forests are an important natural resource in Tennessee. About half of Tennessee is forested. Most of these trees are hardwoods that can be used to make lumber, flooring, and pencils. The Musgrave Pencil Company in Shelbyville, Tennessee, makes up to two million pencils per week.

Pages 20–21

Memphis, Tennessee, is called the Home of the Blues and the Birthplace of Rock and Roll. Music icon Elvis Presley lived in Memphis, and his mansion, Graceland, is now a museum. It is one of the most visited buildings in the United States. Miley Cyrus and Dolly Parton are other well-known Tennessee musicians.

KEY WORDS

Research has shown that as much as 65 percent of all written material published in English is made up of 300 words. These 300 words cannot be taught using pictures or learned by sounding them out. They must be recognized by sight. This book contains 58 common sight words to help young readers improve their reading fluency and comprehension. This book also teaches young readers several important content words, such as proper nouns. These words are paired with pictures to aid in learning and improve understanding.

Page	Sight Words First Appearance
5	from, in, is, it, state, the, this
7	by, of, part, where
8	American, and, for, have, Indians, large, lived, made, more, near, people, rivers, than, that, through, years
11	a, also, and, be, can, has, make, on, plant, shows, to, used
12	mountains, three, white, with
15	animal, are, good, often, they, trees, was
16	named
19	grow, most, these
20	around, come, hear, world

Page	Content Words First Appearance
5	soldiers, Tennessee, volunteer, War of 1812
7	shape, United States
8	crops, mounds
11	flower, perfume, plow, purple iris, riverboat, seal, wheat
12	circle, flag, hills, stars, valleys
15	climbers, Davy Crockett, hat, raccoon
16	capital, Music City, Nashville
19	lumber, pencils
20	concerts, museums, music

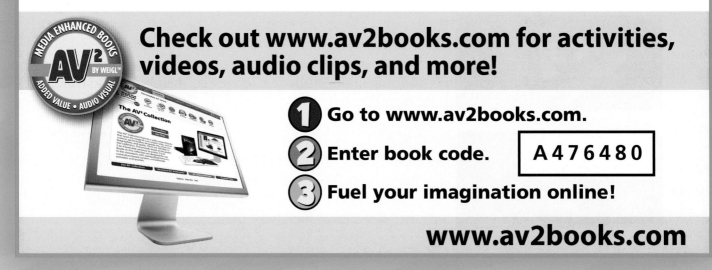